Antique Motorcycle Toys

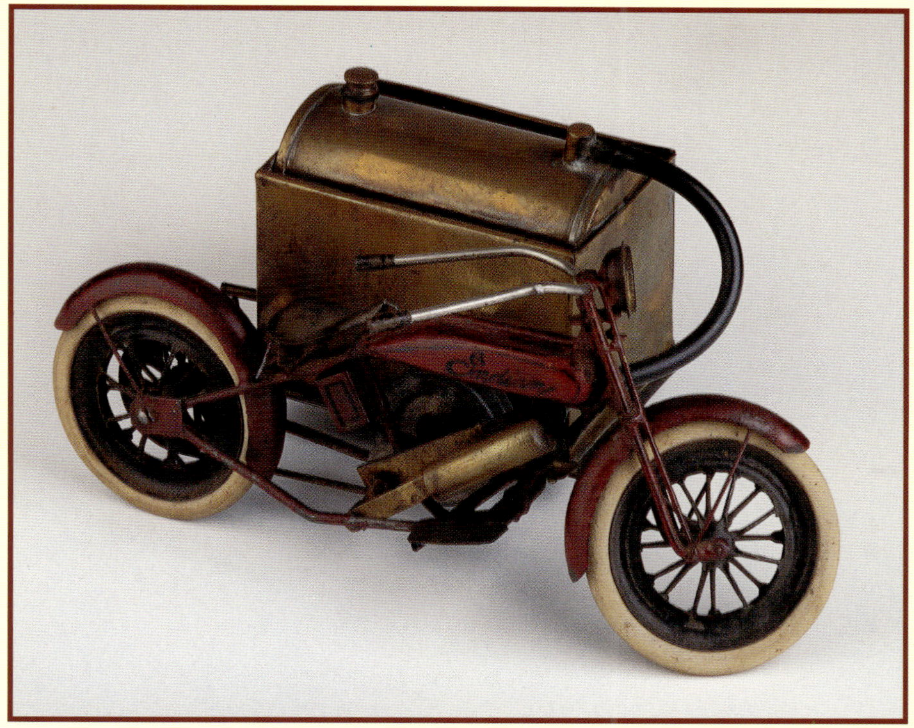

by: Rich Bertoia
Featuring the collection of
"Indian" Al Liebowitz

Schiffer Publishing Ltd
4880 Lower Valley Road, Atglen, PA 19310 USA

Library of Congress Catalog Card Number: 99-62042

Designed by Bonnie M. Hensley
Type set in Milano LET/GoudyOlSt BT

ISBN: 0-7643-0862-9
Printed in China
1 2 3 4

Published by Schiffer Publishing Ltd.
4880 Lower Valley Road
Atglen, PA 19310
Phone: (610) 593-1777; Fax: (610) 593-2002
E-mail: Schifferbk@aol.com
Please visit our web site catalog at **www.schifferbooks.com**

In Europe, Schiffer books are distributed by Bushwood Book
6 Marksbury Avenue Kew Gardens
Surrey TW9 4JF England
Phone: 44 (0)181 392-8585; Fax: 44 (0)181 392-9876
E-mail: Bushwd@aol.com

This book may be purchased from the publisher.
Include $3.95 for shipping. Please try your bookstore first.
We are interested in hearing from authors with book ideas on related subjects.
You may write for a free printed catalog.

Contents

Acknowledgements

Writing this book would have been impossible without the meticulous record keeping, and of course, incredible finds, of " Indian" Al Liebowitz. His exceptional collection is second only to his enthusiasm and passion to foster true toy camaraderie. He has shown me that great collections are made by great collectors, and I hope this book mirrors my thanks.

Thanks also go to my brother Bill for contributing with his knowledge of current market pricing which is essential in making this price guide as accurate and up-to-date as possible.

The entire staff at Bill Bertoia Auctions also deserves applause for their constant positive reinforcement and willingness to help the book's progress.

A big thanks to the people at Schiffer Publishing, a truly professional staff. Thanks especially to Peter Schiffer, Bruce Waters, and Molly Higgins.

Preface

This book attempts to satisfy the reader's visual sense with a variety of tin lithographed motorcycles that are either rare, extremely rare, or in some cases the only known example. It is comprised entirely of items from the collection of "Indian" Al Liebowitz, and he has graciously allowed his beautiful examples to be appreciated by all. I have divided the manufacturers by country of origin, and when possible, the date of production. Without doubt, the German-made examples are executed with most detail in color, graphic images, and internal mechanisms. While the Japanese toy makers were highly creative with their designs, one has to remember that they had plenty of previous German designs to mimic throughout the years. The Germans were considered toy craftsmen long before production costs became terms of endearment to office managers. Unparalleled in their toy inventions, these early designers perfected the art of the scaled-down model, and their motorcycle renditions can almost be viewed as working historical time pieces. Prices included do not reflect the bottom line, but as many other price guides do note, they represent a guide line for the collector. Prices quoted are normally for mint examples, unless it is a one-of-a-kind example, which allows rarity to alter the equation. When purchasing toys, always aim for the best of condition, and let that be your constant guide for collecting.

Chapter One
Cycling Through Europe

The Europeans were fascinated with gas engines, and their unequaled curiosity with mechanical contraptions led to the invention of the earliest autos, and quite naturally, their close cousin, the motorcycle. The first example was more like a bicycle then a self-contained motorized unit, but regardless of its initial primitive styling, the apparent convenience became very popular, and the need to refine its appearance, movements and overall design was a constant incentive for early producers of cycles. Toy makers, eager to ride the wave of motorcycle popularity, and aware of the marketing potential, were also eager to redesign existing models and keep up with the fast pace of this changing commodity. The collection of "Indian" Al contains examples that form a time line of the ever-changing designs of early European motorcycles. I have listed most examples alphabetically by manufacturer, and where possible, the relative rarity. You will note that the Germans commanded a superiority in toy making, and these early toy designers were true masters of their craft. Little, if any, detail was omitted when creating a scaled-down version of the day's favorite cycle, and most, featuring intricate clockwork mechanisms, were made with the same precision as their larger prototypes. Realizing that color also played an important role in luring a child's fancy, toy companies attempted to create colorful renditions using the brightest in tin lithography. This color craze is very apparent in the clothing worn by the riders and passengers. While the cycles themselves were heavy in detail and styling, the human element, depicted in hot new fashions, really helped attract the young buyers. As you will see, buyers today haven't changed much in the way they select their toys. *Color, condition,* and *can't find another one* are still the three c's of collecting, and the European entries pictured in this book certainly meet, and often exceed, those requirements.

CKAO—Trademark used c. 1935

Arnold—Nuremberg, Germany.
Trademark used c. 1950

German and British soldiers riding motorcycles. Both soldiers depicted on identical Zundapp camouflaged motorcycles. By simply changing the helmets and color of uniforms, the company was able to cut enormous costs, and target two different markets. Approx. 7.5" long. Arnold, c. 1935. $600–$800

German military couriers riding motorcycles. Note the similar styling with the addition of a passenger instead of rear rack. These gray Zunndapps with flint-powered sparkling headlights had great toy appeal. Approx. 7.5" long . Arnold, c. 1937. $ 800–$1000

Touring riders. Well-detailed tin lithography, note the drivers are depicted wearing scarves. The original boxes were as colorful as the toys, and although the clockworks seemed awkward, they were very efficient. This model also came in red. 7.5" long. Arnold, c. 1948. $500–$700

The Mac 700 Motorcycle with rider. Very popular to motorcycle collectors, it features an intricate mechanism that allows the rider to dismount after cycle comes to a stop. Pictured in red and black versions, it is toy genius at play. 7.625" long. Arnold, c. 1948. $800–$1500

The Mac 700 with sidecar. Rarer Mac version made in limited quantities, features unusual steering activated by a hand-held injector.
The driver on this model is stationary, and the styling is superb. 8" long. Arnold, c. 1956. $2000–$2500

Performing stunt rider and companion. Curious action, involves cyclist to spin and jump ramp, while companion, sandwiched in spoke wheels, acts a counter balance weight and spins in unison with jumping cyclist in circular motion. Arnold, c. 1950s. $600–$900

Early touring motorcycles. The solo rider has the clockwork attached to the side body, while the sidecar version contains its mechanism behind the seated boy's gondola-style sidecar. Note the detail given to the chauffeur's uniform. 7" to 7.5" long. Distler, Germany, c.1925. Sidecar version, $2500–$3500

Solo rider and sidecar version. The sidecar styling is quite unique. This very rare example demonstrates the toy maker's skills and helps capture a visual history of the popularity of cycling in the early days. Sidecar version, $3000–$4000

Three solo riders displaying their riding skills. The styling of many early German motorcycles by toy makers was similar. Whether they sold and produced parts for each other at times is still unknown, but we do know that countries less industrialized at the time bought many of the German stampings. Attempts to duplicate another factory's successful models may be another possibility. $1000–$2000

Henry Fisher, Nuremberg, Germany

Touring cyclists. The solo rider seems to be making a delivery wearing his red uniform, while the touring pair are road-ready, wearing goggles and casual attire. 6" to 7" long. H. Fisher & Co., c. 1920s. $2500–$3500

Clowns on motorcycle. Colorful lithography and one of many novelty tinplate toys made by this Nuremberg Mfg. The cycle featured exceptional clockwork actions as it was able to perform wheelies while spinning in circles. 8" long. H. Fisher & Co., c. 1920s. $4000–$5500

GAMA, Germany.

Novelty motorcycles with riders. These box structure motorcycles are identical except for the obvious difference in riders. In addition, the monkey performs a quite complex standing stunt while riding. GAMA mfg., c. 1950s. $500–$750

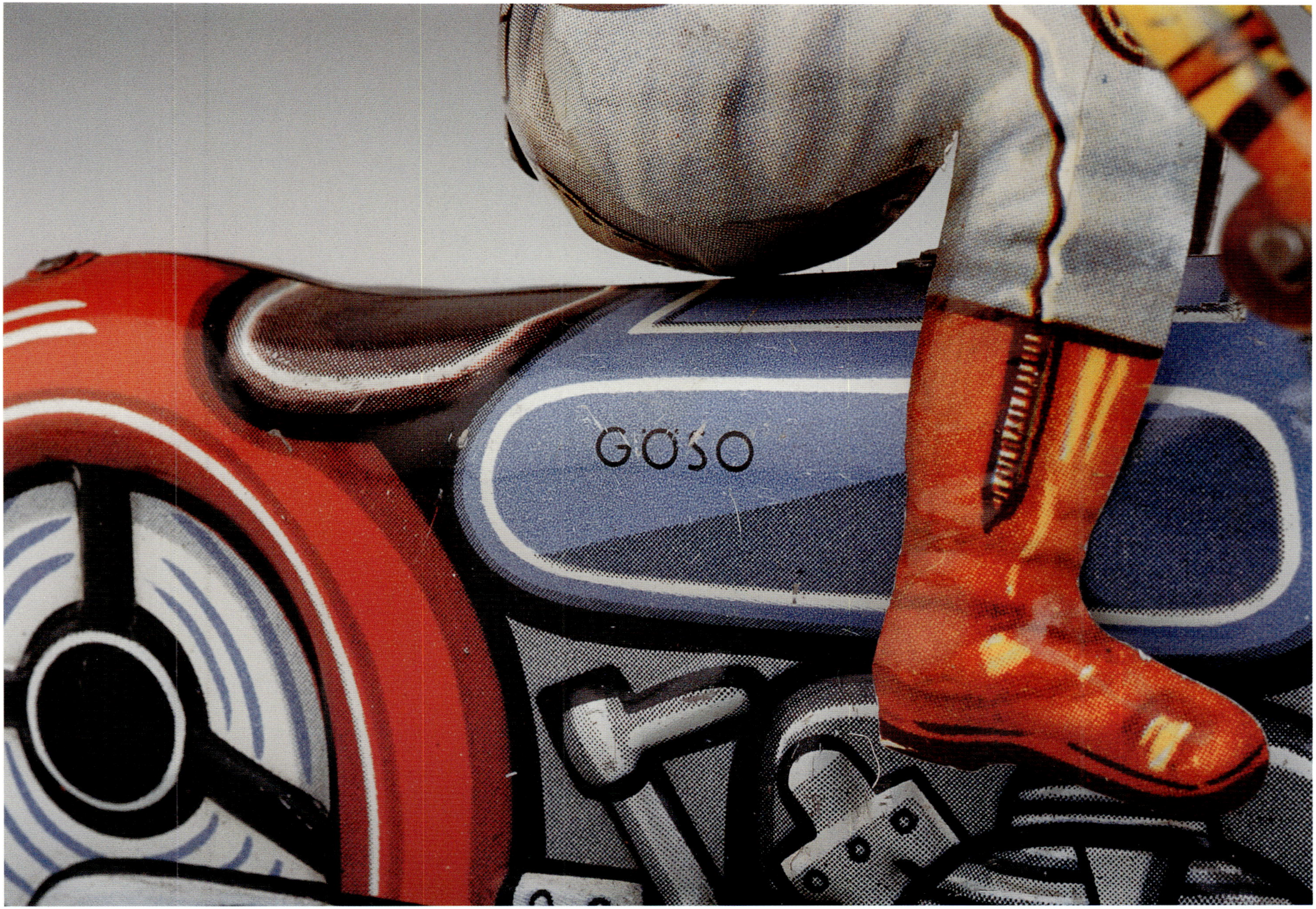

GOSO, Gotz & Sohn, Germany.

Stunt rider. Driver appears to be thrown about when clockwork is activated. Similar cycle design as the ADAC. 7.25" long. GOSO mfg., c. 1950s. $300–$500

ADAC Strassenwacht Motorcycles with sidecars. Sidecars feature opening lids. One variation utilizes the side van body as a penny bank. The composition figure is incredibly detailed. 7. 25" long. GOSO mfg., c.1958. $600–$800

Greppert & Kelch or Gundka, Bradenburg, Germany.

Touring Cyclon with driver and passenger. Exceptional example of toy ingenuity. The lady's parasol actually moves when cycle is propelled by clockwork. 6.5" long. Greppert & Kelch mfg., c. 1920s. $1500–$2000

Grouping of Cyclons. A rare look at a few variations of this well-detailed touring cycle. They must have raised many eyebrows in their day too. Greppert & Kelch mfg., c. 1920s. $1000–$2500

A close-up reveals a Christmas label still attached to rear of sidecar.

Guntherman, Nuremburg, Germany trademark used c.1920–1930.

Opposite page: Touring cycle with sidecar and passenger. Extremely rare example. Hand-painted figures sit quietly on a spoke-wheeled cycle with sled-shaped sidecar. Clockwork mechanism activates spring drive belt. 7.5" long. Guntherman mfg., c.1900. $5000–$6000

Touring cyclist. A well-recognized example. The rider pedals his motor bike as it moves along smoothly, helped by its chain belt drive. Guntherman mfg., c.1910. $1200–$1500

Two more examples of Guntherman's motorcycles, both made of lithographed tin with clockwork mechanisms. Larger one, $2000–$3000

Roundabout Carousel with cycles and fire trucks. Visually appealing with intense graphics overall. This table top toy has fluid clockwork action and certainly prized in this condition. Hoch & Beckman mfg., c. 1940s. $1200–$1500

Huki, Nuremburg, Germany.

Pair of cycles. Similar styling and both cyclists are well-dressed for the occasion. Flapped helmets and plenty of engine detail helped toy designers create exacting scaled versions of the red models. Huki mfg. $300–$400

Moto Cross. Great visual action as both cycles take turns cycling and jumping over the ramp. Curious to note that the base contains flags of many nations, possibly for export reasons. 16" overall length. Huki mfg., c. 1940s. $500–$600

Ingap (National Industry of Automatic Toys Padua), Italy

Touring cyclist. This company used bright lithography, which gives their toys an attractive appearance. 7.625" long. Ingap mfg., c. 1930s. $400–$600

Motorcycle with sidecar and passenger. Another look at the many colors and graphic details preferred by this manufacturer. 5" long. Ingap mfg. $700–$1000

Transport Express Cycle. Making deliveries could not have been easier. It is surprising to me that these express cycles are not used more often today. 7.5" long. Ingap mfg. $500–$700

JML, France

Pair of large-scale motorcycles. Large and colorful, by attaching a heavy gauge bullet-style side car, the toy takes on an entirely new look. Approx. 12" long. JML mfg. Sidecar version, $900–$1200

Ice cream vending cycle. This modified unit features a popular "Glace" wagon being steered by the neighborhood's most popular delivery man. Great scale at 14" long. JML mfg. $1000–$1200

Cyclist with attached sidecar. Many of these cycles were produced by the company between 1930 and 1960. Note the detail of the simple (yet very durable) pressed steel sidecar. 8" long. JML mfg. $500–$700

Pair of French touring cycles. Similar color schemes and graphic details. One features clockwork mechanism to pull its wind resistant side car, while the smaller version is simply pulled along by hand. 6.5" to 8.5" long. JML mfg. Sidecar version, $600–$800

Auto Cycle. Made of aluminum, features a wicker styled side car. Motorcycle is uniquely designed with brass nuts and bolts and clockwork mechanism contained in undercarriage. Jouets, Paris, France—M. Roguefort—Villeneuve, c.1920. $800–$1000

Another side of this cycle complete with twin cylinders and rubber tires over the disc wheels.

Racing cycle. Features driver with co-pilot on rear able to counter balance hairpin figure eight turns. 5.75" long. Kellerman mfg., Germany, c. 1940s. $500–$700

Pair of motorcycles. Two early examples by this celebrated manufacturer. The many colors used on the tourer are truly striking; this penny toy is very stable, employing three wheels. 3.5"–6.5" long. Kellerman mfg., Germany. $400–$600

Outstanding Table Top Roundabout toy. Bright graphics and plenty of action. This rare toy features circling planes, cycles and racers. A definitely desirable addition to any serious collection. Together with the original box, it makes a highly prized find. 8.25" long. Kellerman mfg., c. 1930s. $3000–$4000

Wilhelm Krauss, Germany

Two early touring cycles with riders. A true picture of early touring bikes. Both companies went to the streets and issued similar toy copies. Both are clockwork driven, one features spring belt drive with internal flywheel. Both approx. 8" long. Wilhelm Krauss & Kico mfgs., c.1915. $3000–$4000

Lehmann, Brandenburg, Germany

Touring cycles. One of the most well-known toy makers in Germany. The company produced several similar motorcycles, each named differently. Some earlier models were hand painted, while most were tin lithographed. Mechanisms also varied from model to model, but all were collectively superior in design. Pictures are two colors of the Echo, followed by the Halloh. Not pictured, but part of the company's cycle line, are the Pilot, Quex and Roon. Lehmann mfg., c.1914. $4000–$5000 boxed.

Photo of Halloh Cycle, similar to Echo in all aspects with colorful original box. $4500–$5500

Lehmann's Tri-Wheel Rad Cycle $700–$1000

Billed as the New Century Cycle, it was widely used in the streets of Europe during the early part of the century, and this model had a particularly long production life for its maker Lehmann. $1500–$2000

The amusing Am-Pol Cycle featuring the famous explorer Admiral Peary and his companion Hensley after returning from his North Pole expedition. This could almost be viewed as an educational toy. $2000–$2500

George Levy, Nuremburg, Germany

Couples riding motorcycles with woman passengers. What could be more exciting than riding with your favorite girls? The mother-in-law looks very comfortable in the fancy orange side car. 6.25" to 8.75" long. Gely mfg., c.1935. $2000–$2500

Grouping of military motorcycles. Composition figures and cycles were hand-painted and often sold to many markets by simply changing the colors of the uniforms. Note the intense details of the cap firing Maxim machine gun, and even to the emblems, buttons, and goggles. $250–$400

Mattarazzo, Argentina

Motorcycles from Buenos Aires, the Paris of South America. These cycles show great lithography overall, and each contains a tag which reads, "Ciudad de Buenos Aires." Curiously, three of the examples marked "no.88" have the manufacturer's name on the side, Industria Argentina, whereas no. 48 does not. All of these examples are quite rare. Each approx. 10" long. Matarazzo, Argentina, c. 1930s. Sidecar version, $2000–$3000

Mettoy Co. Ltd., London, England

Two novelty toy cycles with riders. The clown features a hand-painted lead head, while the Indian Chief rides proudly with full headdress. Both are great toy concepts. Each 7.25" long. Mettoy, England, c.1950. Big Chief, $800–$1000.

Two more examples of Mettoy's mastery of tin lithography and creativity. 7.25" to 8.75" long. Two clowns. $900–$1200

Although smaller scaled, these cycles were extremely well-detailed. The clown and the Automobile Association cycles are similar in design, and both feature unusual die cast wheels. Each measures 3.75" long. Mettoy, England. $200–$300

Racer on motorcycle. This Mettoy racer carries the "TT3149" tag, which has been suggested to be the plate used by competitors of the Isle of Man's "Tourist Trophy." We are not sure how this No. 49 placed, but he certainly appears ready and outfitted for any type of weather. 7.625" long. $400–$600

Muller & Kadeder, Nuremburg, Germany.

Touring cyclist. These early cycles were known as peddlers and depict their riders in standing positions. These were the true forerunners of today's motorcycles. The scarce model features a flywheel with side crank and spring drive belt wrapped around the rear axle. This well-preserved example is part of the time line in the development of the motorcycle as we know it today. 9" long. Muller & Kadeder, Germany, c.1913. $5000–$6000

P. Niedermeier, Germany

A Police chase. True toy imagination went into creating this police cycle that actually circles the criminal's car until it stops. Measures 12" long. P. Niedermeier, Germany. $400–$500

The original box depicts these tandem cycles performing figure eights. Unique clockwork actions allow drivers to sway from side to side while riding. Pictured are the Police patrolmen and the racers, each measuring 6.5" long, and made by the Niedermeier co. $300–$500

Spanish racer on motorcycle. Large scale model features battery operated functions. Pictured together with its original box, and original tag. Impressive [illegible].5" overall length, Paya, Spain. $600–$800

Rico, Spain

Couple touring on motorcycle. Well-built model with the same sturdy look of today's bikes. The olive green color scheme is unusual, and not found on many early toy examples. Although it has a rich tone, it may not have been dazzling enough to capture the interest of a child and consequently scratched from the designer's tables, making it a difficult find today. Rico, Spain, c.1958. $700–$900

Royal, Italy

This orange beauty once held a composition dog on its rear rack. The touring rider may have really tested the clockwork mechanism to the limit, and lost his companion canine somewhere in the Italian Alps. 8" long. Royal, Italy. $500–$600

This example was made in Russia. Although not as sophisticated in styling as some of the other European entries, it does however, possess appealing lithography, and a securely enclosed clockwork mechanism. Approx 9" long. $300–$400

Military motorcycle with gun-bearing soldier. This example is a rare find with the complete accessories. This toy company produced several cycles, and all were made in great detail and scale. 7.25" long. Saalheimer & Strauss, Germany, c. 1934. $1500–$2000

Schuco, Germany

Curvo 1000 Motorcycle. This interesting toy cycle was able to perform various patterns by turning a pin on the front axle. This was only one of the many fascinating toys produced by this toy giant. 5" long. Schuco, Germany, c. 1940s. $400–$600

Opposite page: Mirakomat. Another curious motorcycle designed with added attention to the intricate mechanism. The company is well-noted for producing toys with elaborate movements. 5" long. Schuco, Germany. $300–$500

Schuco
Mirakomot
1012
Schuco
Mirakomot
SCHUCO

Schucos on parade. Racers came with different jacket numbers and color schemes. The boxes usually revealed the toy's capable movements, and some examples even have the route patterns lithographed on the front fender.

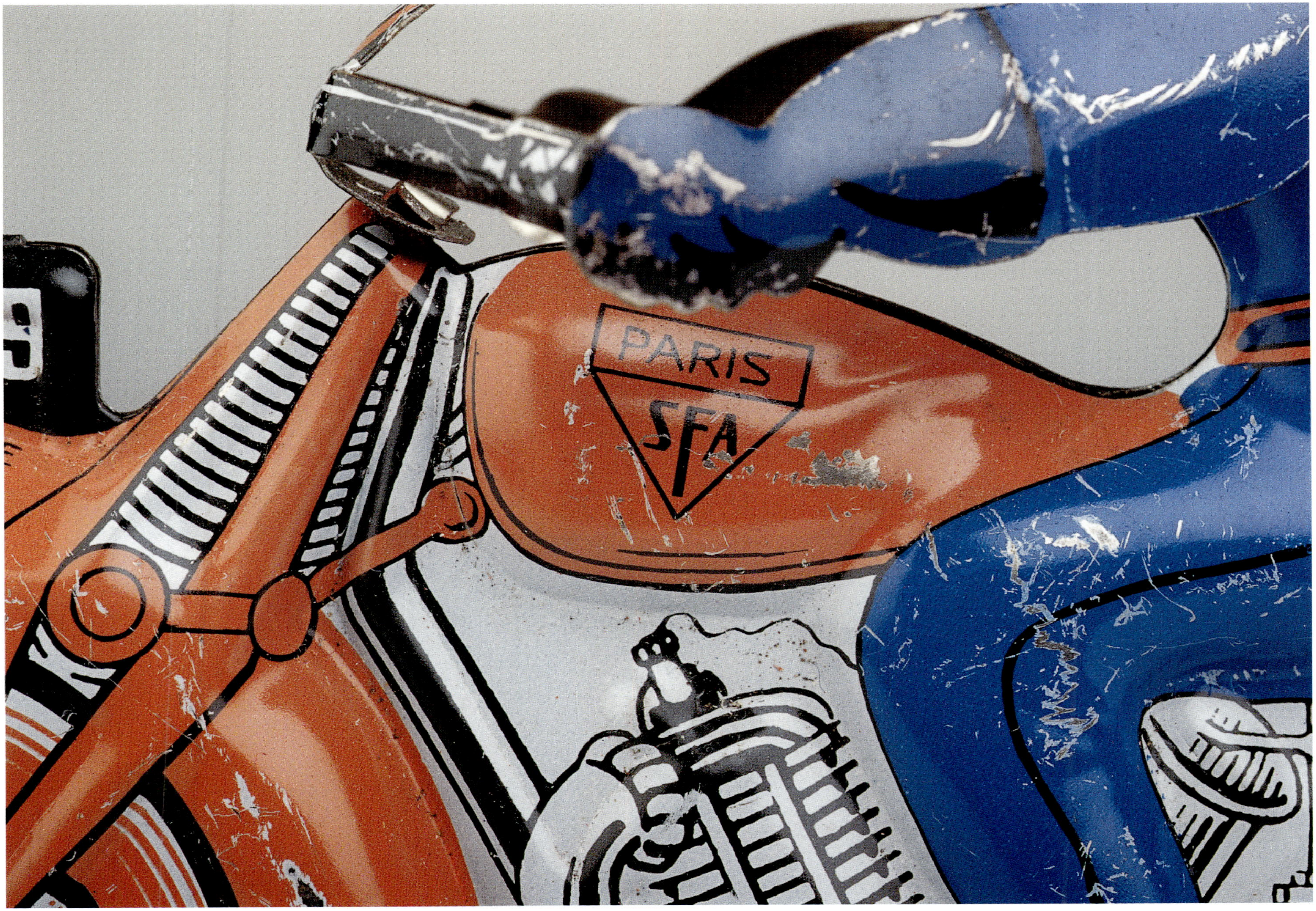

SFA (Society of Fabrication and Assembly) France

2139-RP9
2139-RP9
MADE IN FRANCE

Stock, Solingen, Germany

Opposite page: Two great French examples with similar styling, and extensive engine graphics. This is a perfect example of optimum marketing flexibility. By changing the lithography, keeping the same stamping, and adding a sidecar, the company created an entirely new motorcycle. Each measure 6.5" long. SFA, France. Sidecar model, $400–$500

Woman riding three-wheel Autocycle Runabout. I have included this model to demonstrate the popularity of early autocycles. Women wearing elegant attire found it chic to be seen riding these in the streets of Europe.
Stock, Germany, c. 1915. $500–$700

Technofix, U.S. Zone: Germany

Two racing cycles with original boxes. It is simple to pick out the earlier model, pictured on the right, as its box contains more cartoonish graphics, which were a common attraction with early toys. $400–$600

Assorted Technofix models.

Tipp and Co. trademarks

A touring cycle made by one of the most recognized names in toy circles. Tippco produced a wide variety of toys and the following entries demonstrate the range of their toy designs. They were very popular in Europe and sold many of their stampings to other countries. This sometimes makes it difficult to recognize the point of manufacture for collectors. $500–$700

The Silver Racer. Probably the most popular toy produced by Tippco. It is a true masterpiece in toy ingenuity, as the co-pilot seated on the side sled actually helps to negotiate the turns. Here are two color variations including the very scarce yellow and black suited riders. Each 7" long. Tippco, c. 1950. $1500–$2000

Motorcycle with rider and sidecar similar in styling to the Silver Racer, but featured in green with windshield, simulated upholstered seating, and stylish street fenders, it also came in a very rare battery-operated headlight version which is identical to above photo but not pictured here. 7.75" long, Tippco. $700–$1000

Large touring cycle. Great scale and original box to match. This unit is much larger than most made by Tippco Co. 11" long, Tippco., c. 1950s. $1000–$1200

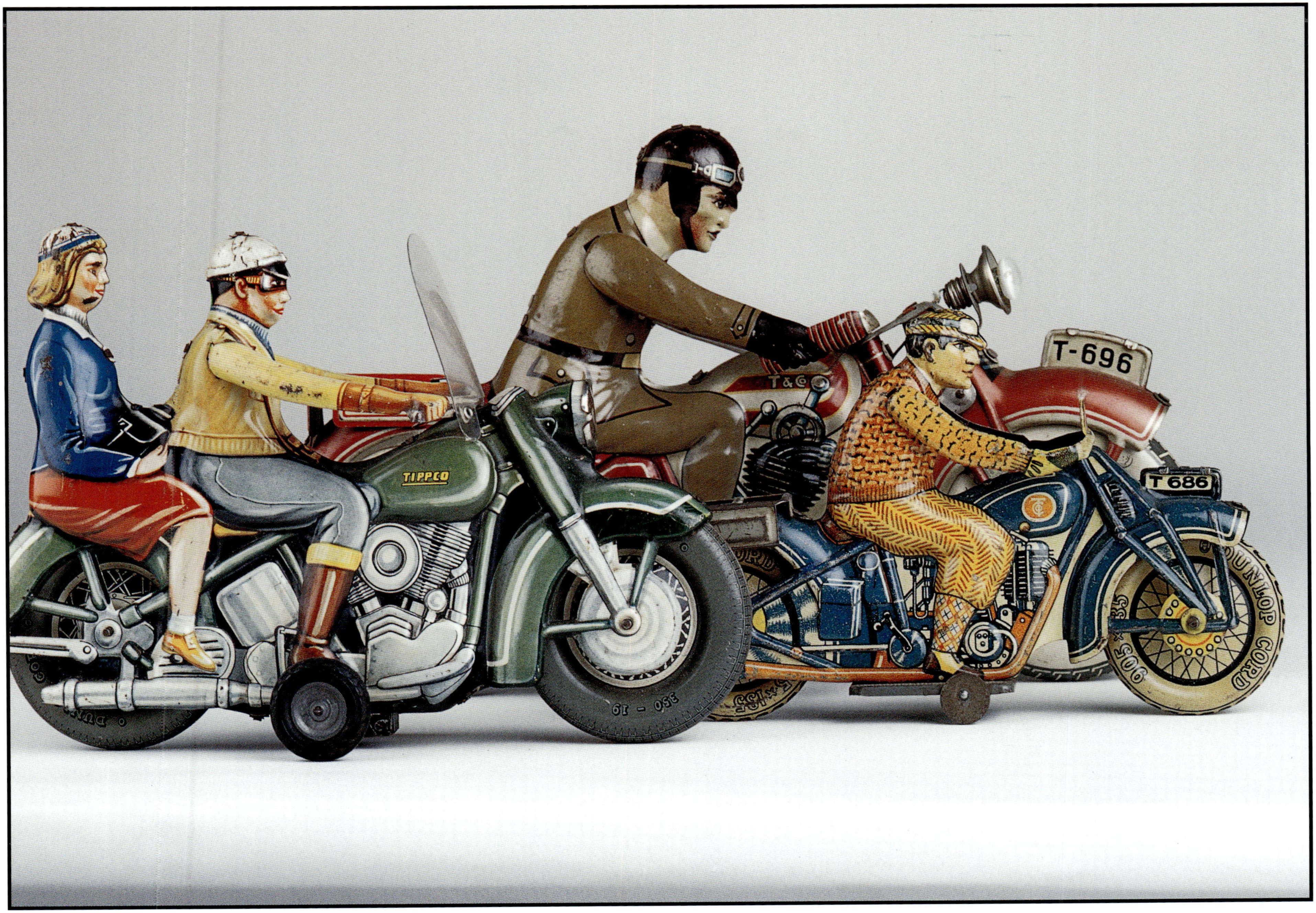

A beautiful snapshot of Tippco variety.

Two Tippco models in different scale.

The popular Tippco sidecar models posing with their passengers. $3000–$4500

Two examples of Tippco cycles, with and without sidecar. Approx. 7" long, c. 1950s.

Scarce motorcycle with composition figure. Rich color scheme surrounds this well-built and highly detailed model. The focus, of course, is on the composition figure, which is fully outfitted in cloth suit. 5" long. Tippco. $1500–$2000

With a quick color and uniform change, these two cycles become quite different variations. Each 11.5" long. Tippco, c. 1950s. $800–$1200

The company suited many preferences by placing or omitting passengers or sidecars.

Two Bella Scooters. Both scooters feature riders with composition heads. The yellow version is scarce, and is pictured with an equally beautiful green model. This cycle also came in a red version with policeman rider. Each 8.25" long. Tippco, c. 1958. $800–$1100

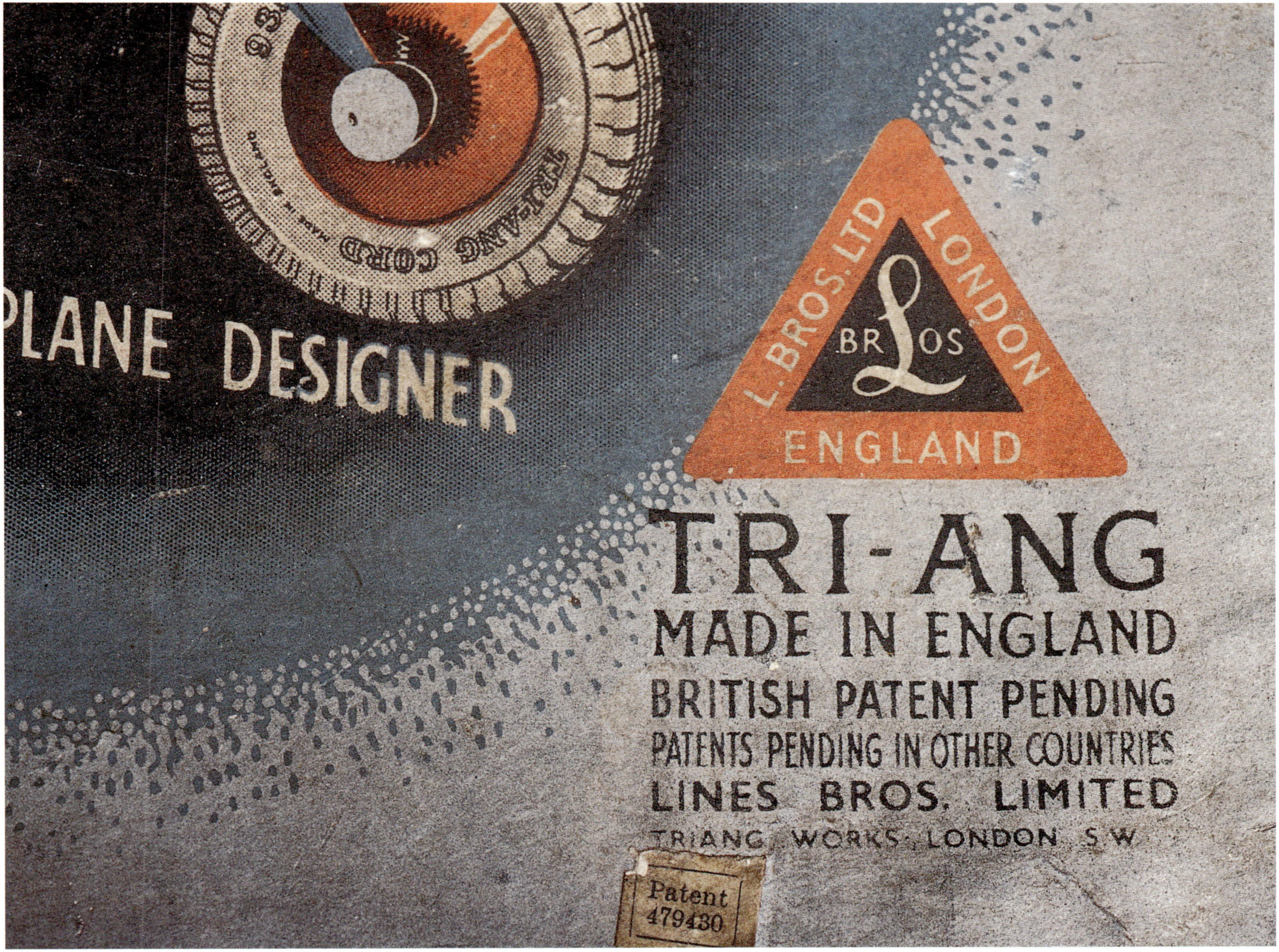

Triang, London, England

The Gyro Cycle. This curious cycle was "invented by a famous aeroplane designer," as stated on its original box. No doubt it contains a highly intricate mechanism that made it one of the most unique cycles a child could ever hope to own. Its gyro actions make it an extraordinary example. 8" long. Triang, England. $600–$800

Motorcycle with sidecar biscuit container. A great concept for a biscuit tin with sidecar lid opening for biscuit retrieval, and once emptied, a distinct child's toy. Made for the Crumpsall & Cardiff Biscuit Co., this was one of many unique containers used by this English firm. This example also comes in red, although the orange version pictured is extremely rare . 7" long. $7000–$9000

Motorcycle with rider. This early peddle cycle is without doubt of German origin, but its manufacturer remains unknown. It is made of lithographed tin and contains a classic chain belt drive with spoked wheels. The original box is just as amazing as the toy: it depicts a cyclist peddling around a track with spectators looking on from the grandstands. This is an extremely rare and desirable example. It measures 8" long. $4000–$6000

A cycle race toy. Another in the unknown origin category, this table top toy cycle race set is made of tin and features two cycles of apparent Meier stampings, encircling the round track with hill in center and elevated base. The camouflage color scheme is very typical of early German toys, and dates it somewhere in the late teens. Approx. 10" diameter. $4000–$6000

Extremely rare motorcycle with rider and sidecar. Hand-painted tin motorcycle done in green overall with exceptional details given to engine which is connected by wire(fuel line) to gas tank. The sidecar also features special appointments such as opening side door and opening top lid. Surely a luxury toy in its day, the spring and gear driven clockwork mechanism place this cycle in the master toymaker's class. 10" long. $7000–$9000

Three little Indians. Even glass candy containers contained the styling and carried the name of the popular Indian motorcycle. It stands next to a detailed hand-held sparkler toy, also of Indian fame, and a German-made Indian toy cycle with sidecar. The glass container is American-made, and accepts all responsibility for intruding in the European section. Sparkler. $800–$1000

Chapter Two
Made in Japan

If the Europeans were known for their styling and intricate mechanisms, the Japanese toymakers will certainly always be remembered for their toy imagination. Having single-handedly controlled the battery operated toy market in the 1940s and 50s, the creations produced were almost endless, and as equally amazing. Pre-war Japanese toys are very desirable today, both for their rarity and their colorful lithography, but the post-war toy trade explosion gave rise to a stream of whimsical designs that kept American chidren amused for many years. People tend to associate the Japanese toy makers with robots and celluloid toys, but their motorcycle designs are just as clever and colorful as any made. You will note in the following chapter that Indian Al's collection features examples mostly from the fifties. This is the period when the large-scale cycles were produced, and generally it is considered the best of the Japanese production years. Enjoy the variety pictured here; hopefully your shelves, if they haven't already, will line up like these photos.

Opposite page: Steam-powered motorcycle with attached boiler sidecar. Although this example has the look of German ingenuity, it has been attributed to Japanese origins. There are very few models of this exceptional caliber known, and owning one like this would certainly take the spotlight in any collection. Upon examination of this piece, note that the piston is steam-powered, and no detail was missed by its creator. The boiler, which was made to resemble a sidecar, is made of brass, giving this cycle a look of importance along with its unmatched styling. Extremely Rare, 6" wide and 8.25" long. $10,000–$15,000

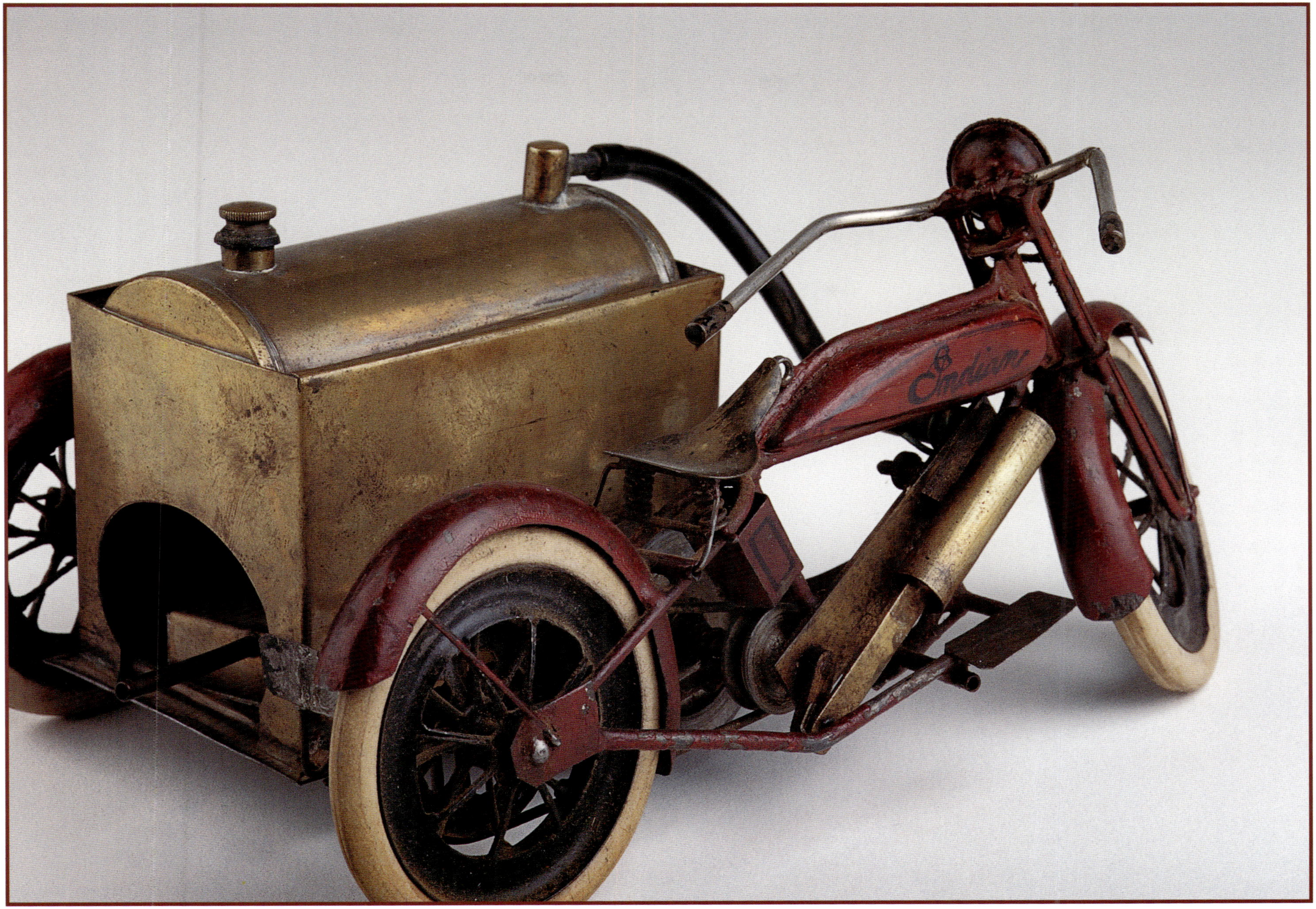
Indian

Top view

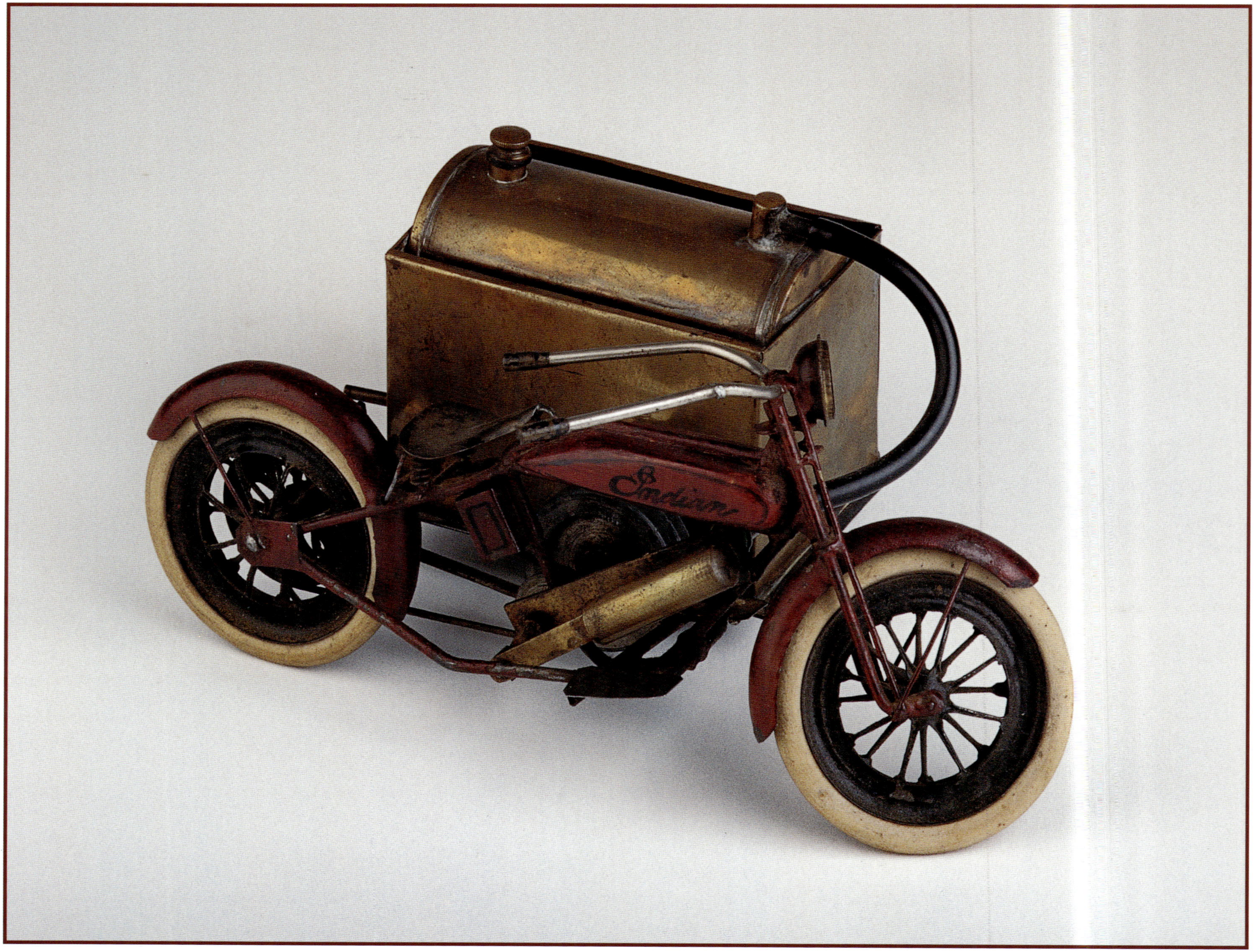

The Romance Cycle. Possibly the most desirable of the Japanese-made tin lithographed toy cycles. A clear example of the incredible imagery given to a toy demonstrating true creative talent. This depiction of a young couple out for a leisure ride captures the spirit of toy making at its best. Colorful, very visually appealing, and together with its elusive original box, is a fortunate find. 7" long. I.Y Metal Toys, Japan, c. 1954. $3000–$4000

Modern Toys,
Masudaya, Japan

Military policeman on patrol. The colors of this cycle make it one of my favorites. It is well-scaled, and contains great graphics overall. 6.75" long. c. 1950s. $400–$600

The following photos show the range of Japanese battery operated toy ingenuity.

Battery operated Expert Motorcyclist. Interesting interior label reads, "Please don't hold me my little friend," referring to its intricate mechanism which allows numerous functions to occur. 12" long. $900–$1200

Battery operated Highway Patrolman along with great graphic details on box. 12" long. $900–$1200

Fire Patrolman on motorcycle. A novel idea for firefighters in a hurry to get to the scene. 12" long. $1500–$1800

Battery operated Santa riding a scooter. Includes many functions, clearly a great American marketed toy. 7.75" long. $200–$300

Battery operated boy astronaut on space scooter. 9" long. $200–$300

Battery operated spacedog on scooter. Each battery-op toy was equipped to perform several dazzling functions including incredible dismounts, stop and go actions, sharp turns, and all with lights and sound, making the toy a complete thrill to enjoy. 9" long. $200–$300

The monkey riding the tricycle was made by Modern Toys while the Martian cyclist was an Akausa creation. 6.5" to 12" long. Martian, $200–$300

Maybe an American TV influence, but depicting policemen on motorcycles was a favorite theme with Japanese toy designers. The grouping here demonstrates a variety of patrolmen on wheels.

A gathering of military minds.

Alps: Shoji Ltd., Tokyo, Japan

A few Alps-made cycles just clowing around.

Haji, Mansei Toy Co., Tokyo, Japan

Girls just want to have fun! Haji made several motorcycles featuring pretty girl riders. $150–$250

Another Haji girl cyclist, and a great-looking Arrow motorcycle with graphic image of tool box and oil can on sides.

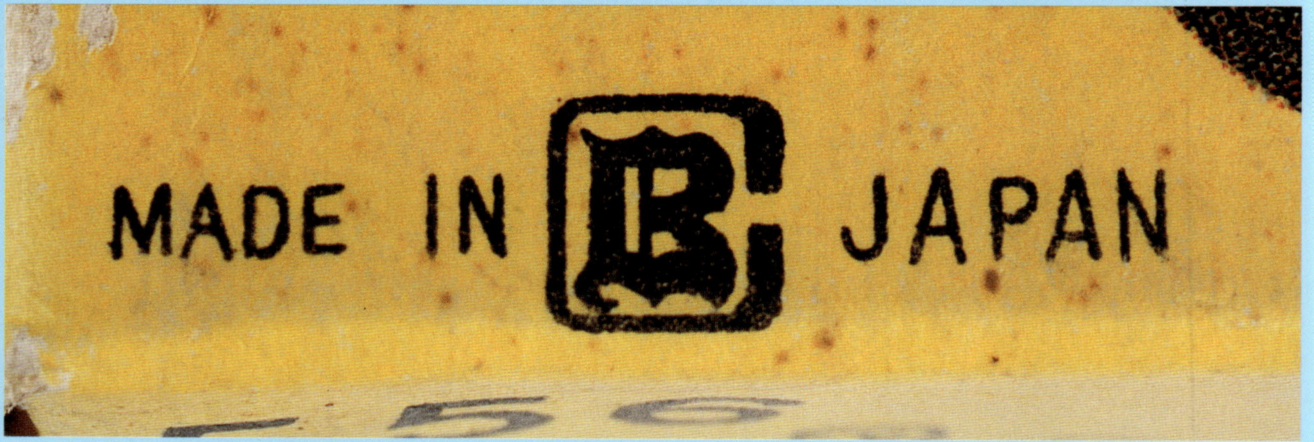

Bandai Co., Tokyo, Japan

Bandai produced many whimsical toys, including the monkey cycle in the center—pictured complete with original box. $250–$350

Another whimsical cycle toy creation. $150–$250

Two examples of putting the cart in front of the horse...power. Left: $500–$700. Right: $400–$500

More horsepower, pictured here in striking examples of Harley Davidsons in red and jet black. $400–$600

Two generic models made in Harley Davidson fashion. The cycle on the right is using an autocycle box as a prop, but it actually came in a smaller box marked "Harley." Each approx 4.5" long. $600–$800

DAREDEVIL STUNT MOTORCYCLIST
REALISTIC ENGINE NOISE
SLOW CIRCLING THEN SUDDEN RAPID PIVOTSPIN
TWIN LIGHTED FLASHING EXHAUSTS
TRADE MARK MADE IN JAPAN
16
DAREDEVIL STUNT MOTORCYCLIST
REALISTIC ENGINE NOISE
TWIN LIGHTED FLASHING EXHAUSTS
SEE HIM START CIRCLING THEN PUT HIS LEG OUT FOR BALANCE AS HE SUDDENLY STARTS PIVOTING
POWERED BY BATTERY DRIVEN MOTOR

Opposite page: TN's idea of a stunt rider. Nice styling and well-detailed wind resistant design. Another great battery operated rendition by noted Japanese designers. $500–$700

Condor cycle with rider. Resembles the Swiss Condor racing cycle, made of large scale with rugged looks, and capable of handling the roughest of road conditions. 12" long. I.Y.Metals Toys, c. 1950s. $1000–$1200

These are less durable in appearance, but were made and built for speed. Note the rear fender area on the Speed Deer which was supposed to read "Speeder." Each measures 5.5" long. $200–$300

Police autos also made for speed; this one is in mint and unplayed with condition. 8.5" long. ATC Mfg. c. 1960s. $200–$300

Group shot of minature models, all colorfully lithographed with fine details.

"Tourist" cycle with enclosed sidecar very similar in styling to the German-made Wegenwachts. The colorful orange sidecar is very compatible with the green attire of the rider. The unit features an opening lid sidecar, adding to the appeal of the toy. 7.5" long. Marusan, c. 1950s. $800–$1000

Japanese toy makers gave as much time to color as the toy itself. The appeal of this delivery cycle is enhanced by its bright lithography. Finding these toys in this condition is a pleasure for any collector.

Linemar Toys, Japan

Policeman on cycle. The graphics on this cycle give the feeling of movement. The overall effects are superior in styling; it was made by one of the more famous and well recognized names in Japanese toy making. 6" long. Linemar, c. 1960s. $300–$400

Linemar produced countless toys, all with very successful production periods. Here are three well-known models of highly recognizable characters. Pluto, Mickey Mouse, and Donald Duck. $400–$600

Another recognizable character made by Linemar—Santa Claus. He is made of celluloid, very colorful and rides a lithographed tin trike which is clockwork-activated. $200–$300

A final entry and the only cycle in this collection made in China. It has all the detail and styling to earn it high marks. $150–$250

Chapter 3
Born in the USA

If the Europeans showed superiority in tin lithographed toys, and the Japanese dominated the world of battery-ops, the Americans can claim their fame in the cast iron toy arena. I have not included cast iron toy cycles in this book because I feel they have already been well-recorded in other books. However, highlighting this incredible tin collection is Louis Marx Toys, an all-American company, at one time the world's largest. A true driving force in the toy industry, they have been included with a few other American notables, demonstrating the capabilities of America's best tin toy designers.

The king of American toys was Louis Marx. They were copied by many other companies, but few came close to their vast toy ingenuity. The Rookie Cop Cycle, together with the Police Squad Cycle are probably the most popular of the Marx cycles.

Rookie Cop. Very popular toy cycle with large siren on side. This model came in various colors during its production years. 8.5" long. $300–$400

Police Squad Cycle. This is a deluxe version of the rookie cop with attached sidecar. 8.5" long. $400–$500

Policeman and military riders. Two more examples of Marx cycles, one has side mounted siren, the soldier has a gun mounted through his armored windshield. Both approx. 8" long. Soldier. $400–$500

Small-scale PD Motorcycle. Only 3.5" long, an exceptionally rare size to find. Marx. $250–$350

Tricky Motorcycles. Both are Marx Toys, colorful, simple, and with catchy name on the box that was meant to attract a child's attention. Each approx. 4.5" long. $200–$300

"Indian" Al's collection would not be complete without these two Indian Cycles made by Marx. Both are well-styled and simple, yet they have great lines and colored for attention. The deep red and orange really seem to highlight the cycles' curves. $700–$900

Speed Boy Delivery Cycles. Three variations of the Delivery Trikes made in different periods of manufacture with the orange version being the earliest, then the red wagon, and finally the simulated wood grain finish model. The company made several other variations demonstrating the popularity of this attractive toy. Each approx. 9" long. Marx Toys, c. 1930s–1940s–1950s. $400–$600

Opposite page: Traffic Cycle Car. Certainly one of the most desirable of the American-made tin motorcycles. Great overall looks and relative scarcity make this a nice find for a collection. Hoge, c. 1927. $3000–$4000

TRAFFIC
CYCLE-CAR
DELIVERY
Hoge

Wyandotte, USA

The Humphrey Mobile is quite popular with collectors. Great graphics and well-lithographed overall. It contains many quirky features such as the outhouse body with top-mounted chimney, which create quite a comical design. $700–$900

The Easter Bunny Delivery Cycle is a perfect example of child appeal combined with a great design concept. Approx. 9" long. Wyandotte Toys. $250–$350

Opposite page: Ice Cream Vendor Cycle. The company was so proud of their design that they guaranteed their clockwork motor for life. They even printed the ad on the bottom of the toy and included a bond in the box! It is, however, a striking toy in more ways than one. Approx. 7" long. Courtland Mfg. $350–$450

ICE CREAM
5¢
ICE CREAM
5¢
ALL
FLAVORS

Amusing Police Chase Toy. Great toy concept features solo cop chasing auto with driver. Unique wind system allows cycle to eventually catch the car and issue an official-looking summons, which is included with the original box set. 11.5" long. Automatic Toy Co., c. 1950s. $250–$350